DEPRESSION & O.C.D.
TIME ETERNITY
THERE'S ALWAYS
HOPE

JEAN
CONNOR
Jones

DEPRESSION & O.C.D.
TIME ETERNITY
THERE'S ALWAYS
HOPE

POEMS FROM THE HEART

JEAN CONNOR-JONES

To order additional copies of this book, contact:
Xlibris Corporation
0-800-644-6988
www.xlibrispublishing.co.uk
orders@xlibrispublishing.co.uk
300259

CONTENTS

Dedicated to Tommy my wonderful fiancé
Sylvia, my precious sister
Tommy, the kindest brother ever and Helene my courageous
sister in law
Also to all friends who encouraged me along the way
Thank you.

THE POWER OF LOVE BINDS US TOGETHER
ETERNALLY

Poems from the Heart

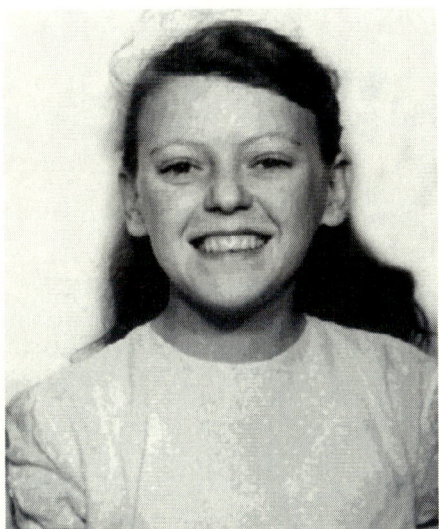

I was born in the back of an old cobblers shop in Liverpool 8. Times were hard, lack of money made mum sick. Not being nourished with enough decent food didn't help her mental health. The house was cold and draughty. Mum didn't go to work as she suffered from nervous debility, panic attacks, anxiety and depression. She was a very emotional woman, took after her dad. Always there in the mornings to make sure her children went to school. Each morning was the same. She got up early and put on an old cardigan kept together with a safety pin. Laddered stockings, kept up with pieces of elastic which left two red lines around mums legs.

After we had left for school she would scrub the kitchen. Her knees rough and red from kneeling and hands that smelt of sunlight soap and soda.

Worry was etched on her face, the face I loved, her blue eyes looked troubled, she wanted much more for her family.

Often I looked at the brass plaque on the kitchen wall. It was called MOTHER. It read

It is a wonderful thing a mother
Only your mother understands.

She works for you, looks after you, loves you, understands you

Anything you do wrong, she forgives you.

The only thing wrong she ever does to you is to die and leave you.

I was afraid. When I came home from school at four o clock I would look for mum. Often she would be in bed. The Librium tablets had made her tired so I would race up the stairs. An old coat was her blanket. Lifting the coat gently I gazed at mum's face, just like a deer that had been chased and hunted down and now she was resting. I traced my finger on her lined forehead.

Depression destroys the person suffering and all those connected. Watching her breathing slowly I remembered those words on the plaque and shook with fear. "Please don't die mum" I muttered to myself, then pulled the old coat up to her neck. She loved her children so much there was no way she would ever leave them.

Mums depression led to obsession and death and destruction were on her mind most of the time. One day when I came downstairs there was a piece of paper on the wall which read "cremate me when I die", she had read about somebody being buried alive and it played on her mind. Mum was only in her forties yet was plagued with depressive thoughts and there was nobody that could help.

She used to say she was tired of looking at the four walls every day.

"Never put flowers on me when I die" she said "it's too late then".

We kept that promise. Mum died at 49 years of age, I suppose you could say she drank herself to death after meeting a man who took her out each evening and introduced her to alcohol which she found a great comfort, but it was an enemy which lifted the depression for moments and then plunged her deeper into the depths of despair.

Her red coat was left hanging in the passageway and I pretended she hadn't really gone.

She had loved dad when they first met but his incapacity made it difficult, he wasn't a well man and didn't leave the house in thirty years, he just stood at the shop door and said "hello" to people, passing by. At three years of age dad was ill with Infantile paralysis which they later called polio. He lost confidence in walking and got around slowly on a metal splint which went the full length of his withered leg. Two holes were drilled through the heels of his black leather boots. Unsteady on his feet, dad was a nervous wreck. A choking phobia meant he had trouble swallowing food. Dad never asked for much, but how I wished he was strong and could take me places but that was not to be. The best he could do was get down on all fours and I would sit on his back for a ride as a child, he managed to go to the shop next door and often bought bars of chocolate and comics for his children. No fancy curtains, clothes or good furniture in my house and I was ashamed to bring anybody home. I was a quiet child who lacked confidence.

Afraid of people knowing mum suffered from her nerves and didn't go shopping like other people and do normal things.

Christmas time somehow was different, there was a roast dinner and lots of presents, I never wanted the day to end. It was later that I found out mum was in debt and was ordered to attend court, but she had made Christmas a time to remember forever. Birthdays were good and I always had a birthday cake, mum tried her best and she did worry so much about her three children after losing her first boy at seven months old. I don't think she ever recovered and was so afraid of something bad happening so I didn't go to school until six years old. Mum didn't trust anybody to take care of me. She was kind and good and would warm the flannel by the fire before washing my face. I never had any vaccinations as mum had read an article in the newspaper about a child getting the disease after being vaccinated. I was afraid of doctors, needles, and hospitals.

I was sick with jaundice at fourteen and mum was frightened and said "if anything happens to Jean then I am finished". I knew from that moment just how much she loved me. She would send a ten shilling postal order when I went on a week's holiday with the church and I always got letters from home even though I was only there for a week, mum never had a holiday herself.

Auntie Dolly was mum's sister and lived in our house. She travelled to Reeds tin factory which was a four mile journey, each day and worked so hard. She would get up to a cold house after being woken at six o clock by her alarm clock which only had one finger. She couldn't afford a new clock but after some months of paying half a crown a week she managed to buy a new one with fingers that lit up in the dark. She would often take bread and margarine to work and we would be waiting for her to come home at six thirty in the evening to go to the local shop and ask for food on tick, it was mostly milk, bread, quarter of margarine, sugar and a quarter of loose tea, sometimes we had a jar of jam. On a Thursday, pay day she would come home with a big parcel of chips and pies. Don't know how we'd have survived without her. She was like an angel and never complained.

Dolly's surname was Owen, her dad was Griffith Owen, a welsh tenor who won the National Eisteddfodau which is a singing competition and is still held each year and I have a medal with his name on.

Brother Tommy, my sister Sylvia and me, meant there were six of us at home. Often we children had to carry a sack of coal so we could all have a warm. If there was no coal to be had, then we burnt old shoes which customers had left at the shop and not collected. It was good to gather around the fire and have a warm, sometimes the newspaper would catch fire against the shovel and the handle would burn. Dad used to daydream that someday he would win the pools and told me to spit on the envelope for luck, but he never ever won. That someday never arrived.

I would go to the local pawnbrokers and choose dad a second hand suit which was in good condition and he was pleased with my choice.

I longed for the day I would leave school then maybe I could help financially.

At fifteen I started work in a shop owned by a Jewish man. Mum would pay him money weekly and I would choose clothes for the rest of the family. My teenage years were an anxious time and I never seemed to fit in. I was nervous and self conscious, didn't drink or smoke and had difficulty socializing, so tended to mix with older people. Two pounds seven and four was my first pay packet. I bought a plastic tablecloth for two and sixpence which had pretty flowers on. Maybe next week I would buy a glass sugar bowl with three little feet on. I bought a roll of black and white linoleum which was cut into small pieces and put on the stairs. Wallpaper came next as I did hate the bare walls, so I set about decorating.

It became evident that I was worrying excessively about so many things.

Putting the glue on the paper, bits of hair were going from the brush onto the wallpaper and I felt anxious. These hairs would be under the wallpaper forever and I worried about it. Carefully I would remove the hairs and this would decrease the anxiety. It went from one thing to another.

Things had to be done in certain ways and I would keep doing them until I thought they were perfect enough. Didn't realize then that this condition would control my life, didn't even know it was a condition until many years later I was told it was obsessive compulsion disorder. Depression had led to obsession and I was always anxious.

Walking past shops I would often have to go back and check various things in the window. Light switches were turned off and on many times until I was satisfied and numbers played a big part in the condition. I hated to say goodbye. Compulsive checking had led to compulsive hoarding. This led to compulsive washing which often mean me washing my hands up to eighty times a day.

So much unrest and torment every day and sleep became my best friend, then I could have some peace, which was my heart's desire. Tablets were a crutch and I found it hard to come to terms with life and death, time and eternity, what did it all mean and how would I survive.

Why was I here? Why was my mother in so much turmoil? Why do people have to be sick and die? Why do things have to end?

The book contains many of the answers I found and which come in the form of poetry.

BROKEN, ENDINGS ARE BEGINNINGS, ONLY ON LOAN, HOPE, TIME, THE ANSWER and FIRST LOVE are among the many. Even some funny ones like THE INNER CITY CAT and LONG IN THE TOOTH.

A broken seed can become a beautiful rose, broken clouds can bring life giving rain, broken wheat makes bread and the cord that is broken and torn brings birth.

Things had to be viewed from a new perspective.

HOPE

Poems from the Heart

The circle of hope rotates never ending
The circle of HOPE
This message is sending
Never give up, keep trying we'll win
Don't stop believing, never give in
The caterpillar struggles to be free
A butterfly emerges, what a sight to see
Colours of the rainbow
Glittering in the sun
He didn't give up, HOPE has won
Looking down at what he used to be
There's a broken cocoon
It was worth all the fight
When morning has broken
'THERE'S LIGHT'
The cord is cut and torn, a child is born
Seeds sown, bring a harvest so sure
Hope from the heart is eternal and true
Mixed with love and with faith
It will bring us all through

GRIFF OWEN (Grandad)

Welsh musicians from Merseyside and north Wales are to hold a memorial service at the graveside of the late Mr. Griffith Owen, the Welsh Caruso who died recently in Liverpool. Choral choirs will sing anthems and hymns and soloists will sing Mr Owens favourite solos. Mr Owen delighted thousands with his remarkable tenor voice and won many prizes at Eisteddfodau.

Liverpool Echo August 6th 1938

Auntie Dolly and Mum with watch on wrist

POVERTY

They say poverty
Is part of our society
Doesn't seem that way to me
Remembering yesteryear
Cockroaches to chase away
No money on Bally-Anne day
No food on the plate
No fire in the grate

Five of us in one bed
Coats for blankets over the head
No carpets on the floor
Just an old draughty door
No fridges, gas fires
Washing machines
They were impossible DREAMS
We lived on tick, burned old SHOES
Thought some day
We would win the pools
A quarter of coal, dragged in a sack
Candle for light and a lav in the back
Poverty, part of our society
It doesn't seem that way to me

79 Upper Warwick Street LIVERPOOL 8 (my birthplace)

Albert Edward Connor (Dad)

FIRST LOVE

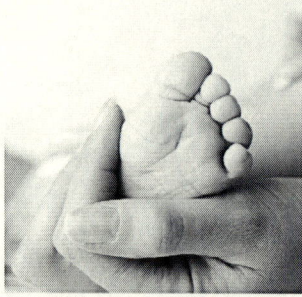

FIRST to kiss me Hold me tight
Sit with me all through the night
FIRST to say to me WELL DONE
Dont give in try hard youll win
FIRST to be my best friend
I know her love will never end
This is the woman Ill never forget
Her love is engraved in my heart
An angel in disguise
A gift from GOD above
MOTHER precious mother
MY FIRST LOVE

Dear Tom Jean & Sylvia

Please Forgive me for the
things I have said to
you I do not mean it
I love you all too much
but life has got me
down I have suffered
mentally and PHISICally
I may not come Home
any more as I dont

cant stand it as
my love always
Remember me I was
very Sick THIS
morning
Take no more of
it never worry it
will do you no
good as I Have
never stopped
worrying myself

Mum came home two hours later

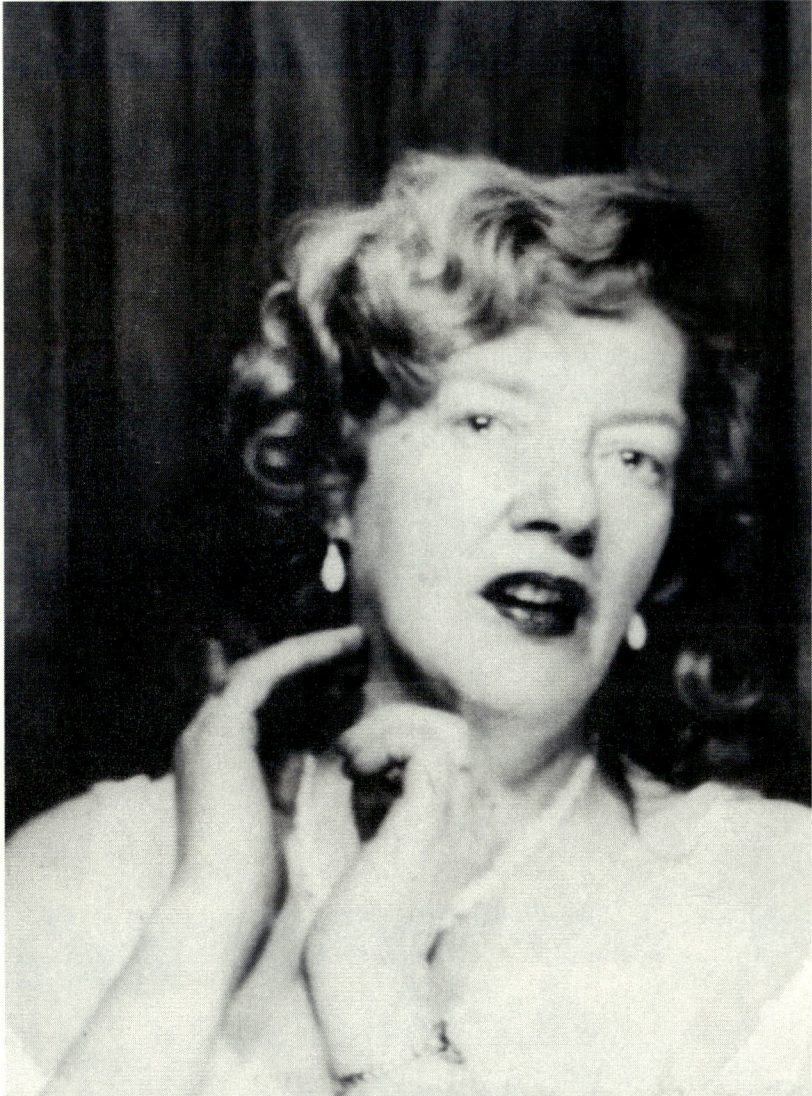

(Jane Elizabeth Connor (mum)

THE LIST

Half a crown each week
The camp seemed far away
I looked forward to my first holiday
Afraid of being away from home
Yet in my heart I longed to roam
Surely there's more to life than this
Buses passing my door each day
What if I don't have clothes to wear
I started to sweat, worry and fret
Money was scarce, an empty purse
I read the list again and again,
Raincoat, strong shoes, pyjamas
What will I do?
Only have pumps not shoe
Wellingtons, swimsuit, towel
Ours are torn
Started to wish I'd never been born
Half a crown a week, then money to spend
That LIST never comes to an end
Mum pleaded with the credit man
"Give me a twenty pound check
if you can"
My daughter's first holiday
He said "yes" and I went away

Me second from the left on the front row linking teacher

INNER CITY CAT

Inner city cat
I'm an inner city cat
My inner city bed is a
Cardboard by the door
My inner city blanket
An old coat on the floor
My inner city wall
Where among the glass I walk
Hearing inner city woman
With their inner city talk
"Scram" said she, looking straight at me
My paws are cut and sore, I'd love a leafy tree
A comfy bed to lay my head
A fire to warm me through
I have a cold a runny nose, **INNER CITY FLU!**

CONFIDENCE

My confidence was very low
Always looked away
When someone said "hello"
Entering a room
My mood was gloom
They all seemed to stare
Was it because I was there!
Neighbours would greet
I looked down
My face wore a frown
Didn't walk tall, felt I would fall
One day I met a girl
Who told me what to do, she said
"There's nobody like you"
Hold your head high
When others come by
Walk with pride
Quicken your stride
Speak slow and clear
This is what you must do
CONFIDENCE will come to you

BROKENNESS TO WHOLENESS

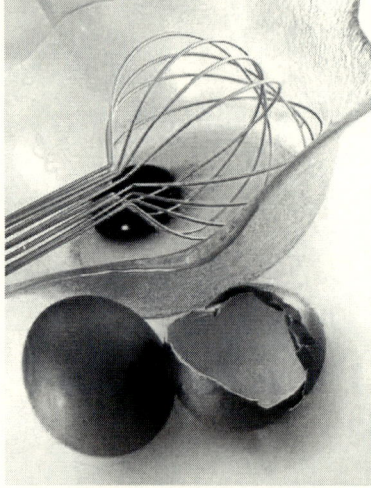

Broken dreams . . . .
Thought I'd be famous
On stage in pink, look at me now . . . .
Chained to the sink
Kids are a nuisance
Nappies they STINK!
Broken hearts,
When will they mend?
The sickness, the pain
When will it end?

I searched for an answer, found it today
Things do get broken, there's no other way
If the cord hadn't torn, I wouldn't be born
My broken egg shell
Gives a yolk that is tasty
If clouds didn't break, how would it rain?
If no one broke wheat
What bread would I eat?
This table and chair, I'm using with glee
Simply because of that BROKEN TREE

COMPULSIVE CHECKING

Poems from the Heart

So many things began to cause me anxiety and letting go was hard. Sending greeting cards had once been a joy and I loved to remember people on special occasions. I would walk around the shops for hours making sure the verse was suitable. It was hard to find the perfect card. Studying the pictures I started counting things, many things, maybe how many cats were sitting on the wall, how many strips of wood made up the fence, how many people were there on the card, then the counting would go to little pieces of cardboard around the edge where the card had been cut in the factory, did this mean somebody's life was hanging on a thread? When writing the message I would be worried about little bits of fluff being transferred from the pen to the card and then going to the person's house. The writing worried me,(if I had forgotten to dot the i or cross the t) I would feel anxious. Worried about the stamp, which I had licked, would food I had been eating have gone under it? I would often throw cards away to bring the anxiety down. Once I had let go, it would be too late and I remembered a time when I had waited for the postman and asked for the card back. That was so embarrassing and I didn't get it back, but at least I had tried which made me feel a little better. Combing my long hair at work caused me stress and when throwing the hair away I was afraid it would go down a hole in the old brown lino so would wrap the hair in a tissue and take it home with me. Dog hairs were a worry if they were on my clothes, what if they went in a parcel. These obsessions were making me depressed and I never got any rest in my head.

Endings were persecuting me. I started to hoard to bring the anxiety down a little. There were certain things I had to surrender and let go, money, prescriptions, receipts and various other things. I would often have to go back to shops and buy another item, maybe something I didn't want, just in the hope of getting my ten shilling note back. I would come out in a hot sweat when I had to throw things away, potato peelings, wrappers from food just rubbish, but it had to be thrown away. I feared going to work in case the bin was emptied and grains of salt on my fingers were giving me stress so I started to eat crisps with a folk.

One Christmas eve I was at the bottom of the rubbish shoot where I lived, looking for something of no worth when a pile of rubbish nearly hit me on the head. People were outside in the street singing and enjoying themselves. One two three four five, I was always counting. Numbers, words and songs were going around in my head and I would write the words with my eye balls until my eyes were in pain. I made excuses to go back to shop windows and look again because I was not sure of the price of some object or another, was it two pound five shillings or two pounds five shillings and eleven pence I would think, had to know or there would be turmoil in my mind . Worried about colour of the fifth jumper on the left in the shop window was it brown or pink? Back I would have to go once again and make sure and then it would be something else, on and on the checking went and it was difficult to get home at times. One day I gave rags away and couldn't go to work as I had to search the rag yards to get my pink housecoat back thinking one of the buttons was hanging on a thread when it was given away. A man said he would save me one when it came in, but I didn't need one. There was a new one in my wardrobe but I needed that pink one back to bring my anxiety down. Bought a set of towels for a wedding gift and how I worried after giving them away, maybe as time went by I would forget but I didn't so had to buy a set similar and go to my friends house making some excuse and asking if I could change the new set for the previous ones I had given her. One day I bought Sylvia a television from a city store and when nearly home I was in a state of anxiety over the way the notes had been folded and given in, so had to rush to the bank and draw money out, then go back to the shop and ask the assistant if she would change the money for me and she said she would. I paid so much attention to detail and was never able to relax.

One day I was in the cemetery and worried about a leaf which was blowing away as I feared it might go down a hole so I chased it and fell over fracturing and dislocating my finger and ended up in the hospital. The knuckle is still much bigger than the other hand, a constant reminder of the depths the condition can take.

COUNT AND CHECK

Reading a book I count
Commas and full stops
"How many are there"?
So much worry and care
"Don't give me that key"
Dropped on the floor
Might have gone in dog pooh
I will wait outside for you
Building houses, foundations
Cements on the stir
Must cross the road
Afraid to lose a hair
It will go underground
Be stuck beneath the floor
Doctor didn't understand
I wouldn't shake his hand
"Take tablets" said he
Never heard of
O.C.D.

O.C.D. WHY ME

Touch, touch, touch,
Check, check, check
One thousand five hundred
Sixty three
Using tissues to touch TV,
Radio, light switches,
Gas fire and phone
Is the cooker off or on?
Is the door open or shut?
Conversation "what did she say"?
So time consuming, I'm always late
Must go through the bin
Which bag did the apple core go in?
Washing hands until red and sore
Who's knocking at my front door?
Visitor might have stepped in dog pooh, I won't open it
Then nothing will go on my floor
Thoughts going round in my head
Every day
Obsessive compulsive disorder they say

CONTAMINATION

Poems from the Heart

The fear of contamination must have come from mum, I remembered her saying she never gave her children dummies because they might fall to the floor and then be put back into the child's mouth. I was germ conscious as a child and when class mates offered me a bite of pink spearmint chew with all the dimples in, I always refused especially if the child had green candles dripping from the nose. When I ate a piece of toast then the piece I had been holding was thrown away. No vaccinations for me as mum had read an article concerning somebody catching the disease after a vaccination and it made her afraid. I worried a lot about dog excrement after reading an article in a newspaper about people becoming blind and I was always careful about shoes especially the ones with laces that trailed the floor, pram wheels and bicycles. Long skirts that brushed the stairs and anything that dropped on the floor had to be washed or thrown away. Shops with dog pooh outside were avoided. There seemed to be dog pooh everywhere I went. The post coming through the letter box and going on the dirty floor, how did people then put it on the breakfast table by their food? I had a box put on the back of the front door to collect the post. Dirty clothes must not touch clean clothes as they would be contaminated. People visiting was a problem, where had they trodden, even them taking their shoes off wasn't enough as their hands might touch the soles when shoes were removed and then touch things in the house.

It was common for me to touch door handles, light switches and lots of things with tissues, elbows or whatever was available. One day I fell off the bus because of not touching the hand rail. Touching taps with dirty hands was difficult as it didn't make much sense to wash dirty hands and then put the clean hands on the same tap to turn the water off. I would use the washing up bottle or a dishcloth or whatever was available to turn the tap on, wash my hands then turn the tap off with my elbows. I got tired of using elbows to open and shut doors and started to wear long sleeve tops to cover my hands when I touched anything. If dog—pooh was outside the front door I was in a panic, how could it be cleaned up, I would go to the corner shop and ask for a cardboard box, then tear a piece off the lid to make a shovel and it could be thrown away without me touching it. How I would long for a heavy downpour to give the street a good clean. I stopped wearing a watch and had a curly perm so I could wash my hair and leave it. Combs were washed and washed under the tap but hairdryers were not used as the wires trailed the floor. Wearing rubber gloves helped and sometimes I would leave them on most of the day, even to read the newspaper, they were so hot to wear especially in the summer. Tissues were a constant companion and I went through boxes and boxes. Even scratching my hair caused me stress because when tiny pieces of dandruff fell I would count them and would continue until I got to a certain number (whichever number calmed me down at the time). Sometimes the bits were so tiny I wasn't sure if they were there or not, so all the clothes I was wearing would come off and go in the washing. Wash, wash, wash, hands then body then clothes, I was tired. It would sometimes be eighty times a day for hands and sometimes seven times a day in the shower, was worried if I hadn't taken my ring off in the shower and washed under it as that part of my hand would still feel dirty.

Going to the launderette was a nightmare, I was afraid the dirty clothes would touch my hands or the side of the washing machine knowing the clean clothes would have to come out of the same hole and they would be dirty again. I used gloves to put the washing in, then put the gloves in the machine and shut it with my elbow. One day I had thirty three gloves in one wash, don't know what happened to the odd one (probably thrown it away). The plastic bag would be thrown in the bin as the clean clothes could not go back in it. I still wasn't satisfied and would then go to the pub and wash my hands over and over again and sometimes to three pubs. Somehow I managed to wash the clothes and knew there was no way of going back again to wash them as there was no cash left, next time I would use a different machine. It was impossible to own my own washing machine as I would be tempted to wash the clothes again.

Many things were thrown away because of contamination and it did hurt because I was a hoarder by nature. Some of the items were dishes, cutlery, clothes and lots of other good things. I stopped wearing a watch as it couldn't be immersed in water and only bought clothes that were washable, stopped using a handbag and used a plastic bag which could be thrown away, when I arrived home.

I was tired and longed for peace of mind so I used tablets as a sedative, sleep was my friend. I would sleep my life away and found it easier to stay in bed.

MAYBE

Caged like an animal
Depression, anxiety, O-C-D
HIDING FROM REALITY
"Take the tablets"
The doctor said
Sleep is my friend
Spend all day in bed
Will this illness always remain?
Will I ever be sane?
Caged like an animal
Pacing the floor
Life is no more
Fear grips like a vice!
Maybe, someday
I will take flight
Like a bird in springtime
Maybe someday
PEACE will be MINE

BETHLEM HOSPITAL . . .

Beckenham Kent

Poems from the Heart

It was now 1990, I was forty six years old and still suffering with O. C. D. when would it end or would it go on forever? I was referred to the Bethlem Hospital in Kent which meant me taking a train to Euston Station then two more trains on the underground and a bus, it was a long journey but I had to give it a try. I was in Euston station washing my hands and the pair of shoes I was wearing were taken off and put in a waste bin. Had to make a good start, or so I thought and couldn't transfer anything from home to the hospital. The nurses and care workers understood the illness but it was hard for me to get across to them the severity of my condition. I had always had difficulty explaining myself.

They made it clear that I had to make progress or leave for home. A programme was arranged and it had to be followed. The programme read like this . . . .

31/3/90
1. File nails daily for two minutes. Allow bits to settle on clothes.
2. I will not wipe my hands or mouth with my flannel.
3. Each time I wash my hands I will contaminate them with my hair and door handle and I will wash them no more than eight times per day.
4. I will wear underwear each day (had difficulty putting things over my feet as they had touched the floor)

5. I will write a letter each day and hand it over to the staff.
6. I will wear trousers every other day.
7. I will wear the same top for two days and take it off over my head at night.
8. Eat buttered toast each day (worried about bits of butter disappearing as it melted on the hot toast)
9. I will read newspaper or magazine each day (had been going over and over the letters and counting full stops and commas so wouldn't read news paper to avoid all the stress)
10. I will give staff a urine sample by 10th April (had feared I had sugar diabetes but tests were all clear)
11. I will eat a biscuit with my afternoon break and bits to fall on clothes.
12. I will touch the floor, then my face ten times a day.
13. I will put my bag on the floor around the ward.
14. I will write a messy letter to Professor Marks within a week.
15. I will write in diary each day.
16. Cook bacon every day (worried about bits of hot oil in the pan and would count them, some were so tiny I wasn't sure if they were there).
17. Eat crisps with fingers (I had been counting bits of salt and was anxious in case I touched something else with my hands and the grains of salt were transferred to other surfaces.

It was hard following the programme but I tried. Walked around without gloves on but I carried a flannel, which was against the rules. In my own room it was hard going in and out of the door. I started to wear underwear and trousers again and let them touch the floor when putting them on.

I wore same top for two days (at home I had been changing my clothes often throughout the day). I wore tights again. Wore a watch again (it had been a long time since I had worn a watch). I used a handbag once again (instead of a plastic bag, which could be thrown away. Used an umbrella again (the other one had been smashed up because it was contaminated).

Started using hairdryer again (not going out with wet hair). Started to go to my brother's house and tried not to worry about the dog jumping up on me. Stopped waiting in the street for Tom to come in (because my own keys were contaminated). Wore long skirts again and had to get used to them touching the floor when I walked upstairs or downstairs.

The staff started to discuss my discharge date and the panic kicked in, there would be a build up if I knew the date and time I was going home. Needed to make a quick exit on the spare of the moment and started to gather my belongings together and without permission of the hospital I left for home. They rang me and offered to have me back but I didn't return. There was just a little progress but I soon slipped back and was not cured.

I did stop staying in bed and got a job as a volunteer in a charity shop (certain tasks were avoided) Some years later I was prescribed the wonder drug Prozac which is an anti-depressant and puts serotonin back into the brain. I f I take enough it makes me a bit forgetful but I feel like taking part in life and it gives me energy and confidence. I did manage to get a passport and flew for the first time when I was 62.

TISSUES

I carry you from dusk till dawn
Hold you tight to wipe my nose
Wrap you around
My blistered toes
Sneezes you stifle.
You mope up the trifle
So gentle on the skin
Now washing is needed
You are thrown in the bin
When there's no paper in the loo
I search in my pocket
And reach for YOU!

AEROBICS

Nan's figure was good
She polished brass, chopped wood
Left right, her hips would sway
Did AEROBICS the household way
Cooked breakfast, lunch and tea
No microwave, remote T.V.
She didn't visit the gym and pay
Did AEROBICS
The household way
No pumping the iron
Nan's was heavy and black
Laundered shirts every night
Collars and cuffs starchy and white
No cholesterol, obesity
She did aerobics the household way
Lived till she was ninety three!

CHOCOLATE DEVINE

Harvesters reaching high
Cocoa beans, falling
Gatherers, catching
Cocoa beans laying in the sunshine
CHOCOLATE DEVINE
Tired hands, shoeless feet
Singing as they work
Cocoa beans are God given
Time to share, pay better wages
Show that we care
CHOCOLATE DEVINE
"Give me more, Give me more"
When it melts in the mouth
REMEMBER THE POOR!

TIME

Sunset—Sunrise
Night becomes DAY
Minutes Hours tick away
Clocks rotating never waiting
Seasons come and GO
SPRING, daffodils, awake
SUMMER, sunflowers growing tall
AUTUMN, crispy leaves fall
WINTER, icy frost and snow
The tide is turning, babies grow
Teeth, multiply
FIFTEEN, a child no more
TWENTY ONE, Key to the door
Age forty, mid-life crisis.

Sixty five, retirement, hair receding
Teeth make an exit from gums
FATTER TUMS
CIRCLES, CYCLES
Constantly rotating, never waiting
WHAT DO YOU WANT?
ACT TODAY, while you may
Make dreams come true
THERE'S STILL TIME!

LONG IN THE TOOTH

"Long in the tooth" the dentist said
"Gums are receding, nerves are exposed,
one day they will loosen and fall
You won't have a tooth in your head"
It's age, we can't change it
Gums are bare, when were born
After much pain
They are broken and torn
Smiles all around

When a tooth was found
Soon the mouth
Was filled to the brim
"Smile at the camera"
Said Uncle Jim
Now I'm in the dentist chair
Long in the tooth
I'ts age, we can't change it
Fifteen no more
BUT FIVE AND THREE SCORE!

SUPERSTITION

Some say "if we do that
We'll die" that's a lie
Green unlucky! How can this be?
Green fields, green trees, Green cabbage, peas, broccoli
Green food is good
For you and me
A four leaf clover, a rabbit's foot
Are said to bring good luck
Horse shoes on doors lucky? NO!
A woman knocked on a door
One fell on her head, now she's dead
Don't put shoes on tables,
Old wives fables! Thirteen unlucky,
Not for me, my winning number
On the lottery!!

SYLVIA

Poems from the Heart

I told Sylvia my only sister about my condition after many years. Didn't mean to hurt her, but she was affected deeply and after trying many ways to help she became ill herself with obsessions and chronic depression, even though she had suffered with panic attacks most of her life, then withdrew from social life and lost her friends and employment. We were very close after losing mum dad and auntie Dolly.

Sometimes the bin would be overflowing but she knew that it must not be emptied as there might be something there worrying me and I had to check again, maybe a banana skin or an egg shell hanging on a thread which I had to take out of the rubbish and hide away until the anxiety ceased. There would be bits of rubbish in the bottom of the fridge and if Sylvia threw them away she knew I would be upset. When I was on holiday I rang to say I was worried about the house money which had been left to spend on food, asked her not to use it as I needed to check it again. Fear of loss even affected me parting with rubbish.

The guilt tore me apart. Sylvia had many chances of marriage and been engaged three times but said her love for me was much stronger than any other she had found. She could sense when something was troubling me and tried her very best to help. Mum and auntie Dolly had stayed together all their lives, history was repeating itself. Brother Tommy who we thought would never marry met a wonderful woman Helene and she made him a marvellous wife. Sylvia and I continued to live together. We had worked in the same retail store when she was sixteen and now she was in her thirties and without a job so I encouraged her to apply for a vacancy in the same city store as me. She got the job and was there for twenty three years, long after I was forced to give up. Tablets were her lifeline as each day she would fight the panic attacks, leaving the house very early in order to avoid lots of people and often jumped off the bus before her stop if it got overcrowded. She would walk through side streets to get home and throw water over her head to calm down. Sylvia is my best friend and only sister and I am sorry I ever told her about the o.c.d. but I did keep it to myself for twenty years and unfortunately it spilled out when I couldn't keep it in any longer.

THE ONE

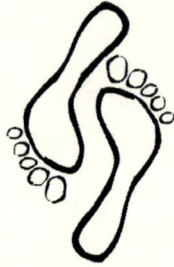

YOU are the ONE
With whom I share
Every blessing, every care
Every giggle, every pain
I always seem to call your name!
THE ONE, on whom I can depend
The ONE who is my greatest friend
The ONE I tell all secrets to
And know your heart
Will not disclose
The ONE who makes my life worthwhile
THE ONLY one
To help me smile!

SISTERS

Two flannelette underskirts
Two pairs of cotton ankle socks
On the line to dry
That's how it started, long ago
How the LOVE began to grow
SISTERS understand each other
Sensing each mood, each fear
Often not knowing what to do
Just being there
Laughter and tear

Even sour moments are sweeter, when TOGETHER!

Shopping for clothes

She knows your style, won't tell a lie

Opens her purse and offers to buy

No other friend can compare

Our roots are deeper than an old oak tree MY SISTER AND ME

TOMMY

Poems from the Heart

Tommy, my fiancé had stood by me. I knew the power of love after meeting him. He was the brother of a friend at work.

I had O. C. D. when we met but tried to hide it and succeeded for a while, my mind was tormented. One day when coming home from Wales

I got distressed and asked him if we could go back and look on the beach as I had lost a hair ribbon, we went back and searched he could see I was worried. We met up every day and Tom never left until early hours in the morning. I would fall asleep on his shoulder while watching television then he would go home and as he crept up the stairs his mum would shout "is that you Tom". She had heard the stairs creaking.

We bought a house together but it was hard for me to choose property.

Tom lived alone in the house for many years and still continued to come to me each day. We had holidays together but it was hard, the checking was worse when away from home. Tommy would keep the keys as I refused to touch them, I always kept the room number at the hotel to reassure myself

I could return if the worry about something in the room was tormenting me. Using the drawers for clothes was stressful (what if some of my hair was left in a drawer) often I would leave clothes in the case. I worried about using the hangers and started to take my own and would often bring things of no value home with me, such as sweet wrappings, tissues, strands of cotton from a garment I had been wearing and other bits and pieces as I found it hard to leave them behind. Eventually I stopped going on holiday.

The loss of my Yorkshire terrier had torn me apart some years before and caused me a breakdown and I swore I would never own another dog but the thought came to me that maybe a small dog around might help so

I mentioned it to Tom and he came home with a Jack Russell puppy, at first it did help but I was unable to cope. Tommy had to take her to work each day and leave her with his sister, eventually we decided it was best she stay with Vera and she gave her many happy years.

Tom became my hands and would do many things for me, often signing my name. I would make excuses for not doing things or going to places because I was avoiding the anxiety. I tried alcohol and it did calm me, but only for a short time, after a bottle of wine I would fall on the bed exhausted only to wake up the next day feeling the same.

Eating food and drinking were very stressful. Having cups of tea was a problem as I was counting the bubbles, the way the tea swirled around in the cup, grains of sugar that had dropped and went in the saucer etc.

There was no end to it. Marks around the edge of the cup were making me anxious. If I was content then I would drink it in one gulp but so many times the cup of tea would be thrown away. I started to use paper cups, stopped washing dishes, hovering, dusting and cooking. Tom did the cooking but we always done the shopping together. I had an amazing man in my life and he was part of my family. My job had gone and I was receiving a giro each week as my payment book had been thrown in the bin . . . . sometimes I had to rip giro's up because of contamination. That was the straw that broke the camel's back and I was referred to a hospital in Kent which specialised in the condition.

Some years later Tom became very ill and went into hospital, it was so dreadful to watch him suffer, one day he put his thumbs up to say I am o.k. (a man of courage who tried to look on the bright side) then he pointed a finger up and said "home" just like E.T. I said three things as he lay ill "I love you" (he said "I love you too") I said "Thank you" (yes I was so thankful for all the years we had together) then said "I am sorry" (I was sorry he had to bear my condition) but he always chose to stay with me and neither of us could say goodbye. He went to heaven. It was Christmas
Eve when we laid him to rest and on the way out of the church the pianist played Silent Night. It was a heart ache and I hold him close in my heart forever.

TOM

Ten pounds at birth, so bonny
A head of curls when he was three
TOM was lost and someone said
"Hello Shirley Temple head"
Pocket money when Tom was eight
A bottle of milk and a whole malt loaf
He spent the lot, just couldn't wait
Cyclist, guitarist, the army
His eyes were as blue as the sky and the sea
Carpenter, with creative hands
Tom loved to fashion wood
Car mechanic, bricklayer, upholsterer, chef
The list goes on, Dad's favourite son

Tom was my man,
Always there for me
So strong he would lift me high
Then I would sit on his knee
My sweetheart, fiancé, my friend
On him I could always depend
THANK YOU, I LOVE YOU and SORRY MY TOM
ETERNALLY, in my heart you live on

(for Tom)

SO CLOSE

So very close you are to me
Like a branch, on a tree
A pearl in an oyster
A wick in a candle
A key in a lock, a foot in a sock!
I think of you, EVERY DAY
Remember things, you used to say
So close and yet so FAR
But only TEMPORARY
Death is a comma, not a full stop.
Someday we will be
SO CLOSE for all ETERNITY!
For my Darling Tom

ONLY ON LOAN

Only on **LOAN** this house that I own
One day I know, will have to let go
Don't understand just can't reason why
"Wish I could keep it **FOREVER**" I cry!
Only on loan "who's that on the phone"
"We are coming today"
"Your phone's out of date
We'll take it away"
Only on **LOAN**
"My baby has grown"
She will soon be a wife, funny old life
Only on loan, how **TIME** has flown
"My birthday is near
Don't want it known"

Wish TIME stood still, but it never will
What does it mean ONLY ON LOAN?
It means we possess things
But they are never our own
They all belong to the Father above
HE lends them to us
Because HE is LOVE
There is coming a day
We will have to surrender
All that we own, back to the lender

BUTTONS

A small white button from your baby grow
Bright red shiny one from your shoe, age two
Square shape in grey, I keep with pride
From your gym-slip, you were five.
Eleven, secondary school, your first day
I followed you all the way
A button fell from your mac, it was black
Fifteen, growing tall
I found a denim button in the hall
A green satin one, so shiny and bright
You looked beautiful that night
BUTTONS galore, I have thirty four
Some shiny, some dull, big ones and small
A royal blue when you went to the ball
My daughter, now you're far away
I think of you each day, when I'm feeling blue
Reaching for my buttons I reminisce of you

I WILL BE THERE

She grumbled at mum
Hot water wasn't on
Her clothes were not ironed
She was angry and wined
So many things mum had done
Washing, cleaning, making stew
Joan didn't say, "Mum how are you"
Never noticed her twisted hands
Far too busy making plans
Ran upstairs to wash her hair
Mums face was lined with care
Make-up on, "bye mum"
A tear fell down mum's cheek
She found it hard to speak
"Bye my daughter please take care"
When you come home, I will be there

COUCH POTATO

Couch—potato arise
Couch potato arise
Raise the arms, slap the thighs
Run on the spot, one, two, three
Stress will run, calm will come
Wave the hands, shake the feet
Dance awhile, s-t-r-e-t-c-h the face SMILE
Put on the trainers, RUN
Drink water for skin, SWIM
Work-out, ride a bike
COUCH POTATO arise COUCH POTATO ARISE
Raise the arms
EXERCISE

THE ANSWER

Home was a doorway
Since Billy had that row
On an icy floor he sat
Clinging to his coat and hat
No duvet on the bed
No water in the tap or dishes in the rack
No table to sit by, Billy gave a sigh
The only thing to do was pray
"Please Lord show me what to do
Maybe I'm to blame, I let the temper win
Never turned the other cheek
Wish it was this time last week
Walking out I banged the door
It's cold and wet on this hard floor"
Billy looked and saw a dove
The answer was the power of LOVE
Kissing doves he won for her
One day at the fair

Anne cried tears of joy, they married
Had a baby boy, he swallowed pride
Picked up the phone "I am sorry" said he
"Come back said Anne come back home"
God answered his prayer
Showed him the dove
The answer was clear
THE ANSWER WAS LOVE

SPRING IN THE CITY

Weeds coming through cracks
On the backyard wall, broken glass
Keeping thieves at bay
Buckets of hot water to chase grime away
A spider floats on a soapy bubble
Having a ride in the sun
Tufts of grass peeping through concrete flags
A group of ants scurry along
Tiny pink flowers
Sprouting through bricks
Flying seeds have taken root
"Must put rubbish in the bin"
No sweet smelling roses in my garden
Just an old backyard IN THE CITY
And it's SPRING

RESCUED

A ship collided
Oil leaked away
A beautiful swan was covered in full
Turned black in the night
Couldn't take flight
"Help me" said she, giving a sigh
Think I am going to die"
A stranger passed and heard her plea
Held out his arms, calmed her alarms
He gently washed her
Feathers turned white, fluffy and neat
Now was the time to retreat
While flying away, she looked back to say
"Thank you for saving my life today"

THE PIP

It started with a pip
She dug a hole and planted it
Fed and watered, watched with care
It started to grow, a shoot said "hello"
Then came a branch, a trunk and a tree
Growing high, stretching it's arms up to the sky
One sunny day rewards came for May
Looking out, she gave such a shout
"Look what I see, blossom on the tree"
NEW LIFE there for you and for me
All because of a pip
She sowed in HOPE, it sat in the dark
Now there's branches, leaves, apples
And the sound of a lark

(FOR MAY)

LOVE

The more we give
The more we retain
Amazing but it happens
Time and time again
Smiles, laughter and tears
All play a part
Memories warm the heart
Kings and beggars alike
Long for a share
Love revives
It's forgiving
Makes life worth living
Every day, give love away
You'll see
Love will return abundantly.

ROYAL

Snow white swans, long necks so fine
Diamonds from the mine
Rubies rare!
Cultured pearls on ladies necks
As they sit and dine
Lions are jungle kings
Eagles with majestic wings
There is someone royal
He came from the sky
Gave His life to set us free
We will live ETERNALLY
He tells us to be strong even when weak
Then He will speak "I made you, I love you
Understand all this woe"
Suffered myself on a cross long ago"
Yes! He's better than gold, or rubies so rare
He's royal, a king and He does really care
Says "I am always with YOU everywhere"

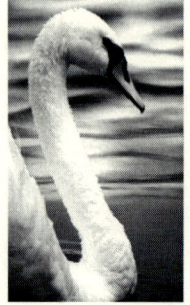

For May
The Lord gave me this poem to encourage her
In the hard times

YEILD

The large oak tree said "look at me
I'm the biggest in the field"
He wouldn't bend, yield
The blade of grass felt so weak
Just couldn't speak
What would he do?
When the hurricane blew
Storms arrived, lightening struck!
The oak tree fell to the ground
Laid in the field
The blade of grass stood tall
Bending, surrendering, YEILDING, he didn't fall

Don't be stubborn
Say sorry, surrender
Was it a friend or family member?
Hurt you so
Forgive . . . . it's so hard to do
Remember, Christ forgave you
It's worth it you'll see
Be like the grass blade
Not the OAK TREE!

JUST DO IT

I bought a pair of training shoes
Needed to lose fat on thighs and bum, but I didn't run
They're still in the box
Next to my socks
I bought a diet book
Must learn how to cook
It's still on the shelf
I have to read it, act upon
To obtain a smaller bum
Put trainers on the feet
Run with haste
Down the street
No good to sit down and sigh
Get up and do it, TRY
Change will come for sure
As we practice more and more
Not what we say but what we do
Do it then a brand new you

SAY NO

I wanted to alight, before the bus stop
Please let me go"
The driver said "NO!"
A dog stepped on to a busy road
His owner said "NO!"
The child struggled
Mum's hand was firm
A building site lay ahead
If he ran in there he could be dead!!
She said "NO don't go"
"Heroin, crack cocaine
Here take and enjoy, there's a good boy"
There is a thrill, but it can kill
After the high comes the low
SO BE STRONG
IF IT'S WRONG SAY NO!

TYPES OF LOVE

PHELIO love is friendship
STORGE is affection
Same goals and desires
Hold on when you find
EROS love is erotic, hot, exciting
Good when with the others you've got
When alone it can cause you to fret
You might be sorry you found it
And down in the pit
AGAPE love is sacrificial
Precious, unconditional and true
"I understand and I hold your hand"
Says the Saviour to you
Many kinds of LOVE
Get them in the right order
Friendship, affection, sacrificial, erotic
Make sure you find
The very best kind

ENDINGS ARE BEGINNINGS

A grain of wheat is buried
Sown in the ground
Is it the end? NO!
SOON IT WILL GROW
End of childhood, youth begins
End of marriage, forty divorced
Children have grown, feeling alone
Begin again, start anew
Do things you've always wanted to do Retirement, on the scrap heap!
Don't weep, make a new start
Learn a new art
Painting, dancing in a line
Cooking soup and Irish stew
New beginnings just for you
End of night, beginning of DAY!
End of year, a new one has come
Yesterday's gone,
It's time to move on.

NEW LIFE

Looking across the field of hope
All looked cold and bare
No daffodils there
A woman stopped she said
"They're dead"
Her friend said "no"
Just fast asleep
The daffs' will wake again
In spring
Stand up tall and sing
Strong again after their rest
We will gaze and be so blest
Don't think they've gone away
Soon they will be in full array
Trumpets bold colours of gold
Many more in the fold
Daffodils don't really die
They sleep then wake and MULTIPLY

LOOKING AGAIN

The world seems BIG, as I look around
Oceans deep, mountains steep
The sun, the moon, stars shine bright
Looking UP on this fine night
So high, so tall, the buildings seem
So wide the shore, so deep the sea
So high the sky, how big that tree!
At last I know what to do
Climb to heights Ive never known
Soar with eagles high ABOVE
Now Im looking DOWN not up
All has changed look and see
Those things that seemed so big to me
Now look small, I feel tall
High up here above them all
Where is that mountain
Wheres that tree?

One Saturday morning I was feeling glum and trying to make sense of life when a programme came on the television about Helen Sharman, the first woman who went into space. She said the earth looked like the size of an orange from where she was. It made me think that all the things I was worried about would appear to be so much smaller from a distance. Instead of looking up I had to look down from God's perspective.

I wrote this poem . . . .

PREPARE

Do you prepare in the spirit?
Before you arrive
So PREPARE, take time, do your part
The LORDS presence
Then will fill your heart
Do you watch t. v. all day long?
Go to church late
Spiritual weak not strong
Look at the ceiling
Betty's new hat, then say to your friend
"This church is flat"
You didn't feel the SPIRITS power
Just slouched in your seat
Looked at your feet
Did you fancy a chat?
Was it somewhere to go?
Were you fed up with knitting?
Too tired to sew
It's time you did your part
If the church closed down
Would you grumble and frown
Don't forget to PREPARE
Before you arrive
Then the church will come ALIVE

POWER

Her watch had stopped
What would she do
Just didn't know the time
Bought a battery put it in
Now the watch is fine
No light in the kitchen
Couldn't cook the meal
Put in a light bulb, 100 watt
Food's on the table, that curry is hot!
Monday morning, time for work
She rushed outside the door
Turned the key in the ignition
The car stuck to the floor!
She couldn't move, what a blow,
Bought petrol, put it in
Speed returned
'That's good' she yearned

"I have NO POWER", I hear you say
In the Christian life, each day
Read God's Word, pray, talk to Him
In the Spirit be lifted high
Like the eagle you will fly!

SPIRITUAL ARMOUR

Put on the armour, each day
In order to live the spiritual way
Tie the belt of truth tight
Lies of Satan will take flight
The sword of the spirit is the Bible
Speak it bold and clear
When strongholds are near
The helmet of salvation on the head
"I have the mind of Christ" say
Wear the gospel shoes
Tie the breastplate of righteousness tight
Christ was made sin
We can be righteous within
Above all the shield of faith
Fiery darts of Satan will bounce off
No protection for the back
Put on the spiritual armour, attack!

THE CREATOR KNOWS HOW

Light life and love, the Creature knows how
Life when we sow light makes it grow
It's all in the plan
There's night and there's day
He fashioned spiders, horse, sheep and cow
Fingers and feet, knobbly knees
Sunshine and rain wind and the breeze
Winter and summer autumn and spring
He gave flowers colour, taught birds to sing
Light life and love, it should have been good
Mankind likes to rebel, made their own hell
Why all the care, all the despair?
Why all the war what's it all for?

One day God will create a new earth
We will dance a new dance
Sing a new song
The end of the rainbow His promise is true
Christ who was slain, lives again
Light life and love the creator knows how
Death is no more, He will restore

GOD HAS PROVIDED FOR ME

I awoke one morning,was just lying there
Said to myself "does God really care"
Looked out of the window
Multi-coloured flowers, freshened by showers
Then the decor spoke
Curtains, pillows and duvet
From cotton fields far away
Floorboards and a wooden door
Made from Gods pine, now they are mine
Woollen blanket from the sheep
Has given me a good night's sleep
I went downstairs, made toast and tea.
Sugar from cane, milk from the cow
Toast made from wheat, eggs from the hen
"Thank you Lord, You've done it again"
Look around and see
God has provided for you and for me

DAD

Dad's build walls, fix toys
Fly kites, drive kids to school
Teach them to swim
Different sizes they come in
Tall and slender, fat and small
"Dad I'm scared, it's dark in the night"
My favourite story, then he read
I fell asleep holding onto Dad's head
If the love of a dad you've never known
And cannot understand
There's something you should know
Your HEAVENLY FATHER up above
Love's you with everlasting LOVE
No evil fear, HE lifts you high
In the Spirit you will fly
He gives HOPE in the storm
STRENGTH for the fight
Underneath are the
EVERLASTING ARMS
He gives PEACE in all alarms

THE TONGUE

The TONGUE in the body is such a small part
In order to tame it we need a new heart
WORDS can kill, destroy make war
Words can heal, build up repair
Encourage someone in despair
Must watch what we say
Might regret it someday
A lion we can tame, subdue
A horse a bit can turn around
In order to tame the tongue, this small member
To self we must die, to CHRIST must surrender
Then HIS church will grow stronger
Light will shine brighter, words will be wiser
When we are angry and the tongues like a razor
Remember loose lips sink ships so they say
That little Tongue likes to have its own way
Do we speak words of hate?
Do we lie? Do we shout?
What's in the heart will always come out
So each day to CHRIST we must surrender
Say "Christ lives in me", I have a new heart
Stop the TONGUE before we start

COMFORT

A duvet, wrapped around feet and head
Brings comfort when laying in bed
The comfort of a teddy bear
When baby feels nobody's there
The comfort of a mother's arms soothes pain
Helps us smile again
After walking a mile
Feet are red and sore
Slippers are a comfort, so soft against the skin
A cup of tea's a comfort
The moment we come in
Jesus said "Another COMFORTER I will send"
The HOLY SPIRIT . . . . will walk alongside
Rebuke, control and guide
Give insight, teach us what to say
We must be refilled each day

STALE OR FRESH

With butter it's delicious, FRESH BREAD
When stale it's mouldy and green
Hard as lead
Babies are cute when fresh
When stale, they are in a mess
Fresh milk, tastes good
When stale, it stinks must be thrown away
We need it fresh each day
Fresh water, fresh meat
Fresh fruit and veg we eat
As Christians it's true
We must freshen each day
Or we'll be stale, hard as lead
Like that green mouldy bread
Feed on God's word and PRAY!
Let the living water flow
Then we will spiritually grow

THE CROWN

No rubies in that Crown He wore
No diamonds rare to shine.
Just rugged thorns sharper than nails
Bent and twisted around
BLOOD flowed that day
Christ allowed it to be
For you and for me
Men said "you're crowned"
Pushed Him around
They spat and they laughed
While walking away
Someday, they will cry
When they see Him on high
Wearing a Crown, bright as the sun
Like the stars it will shine
They will know, JESUS WON!

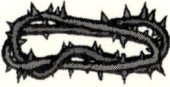

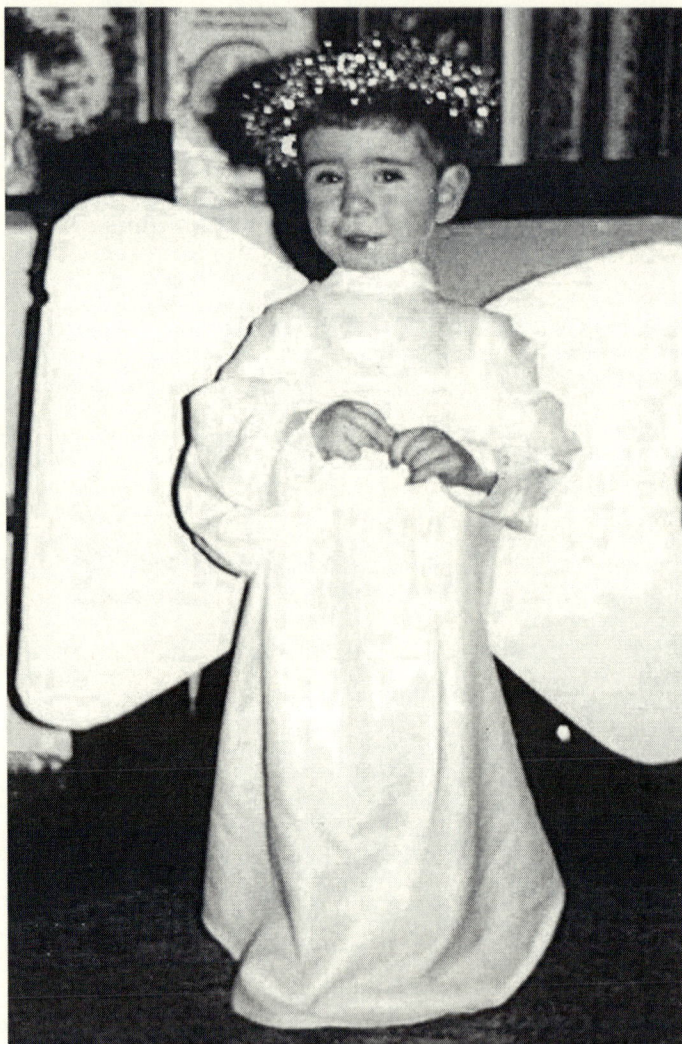

Liam Pettitt
Little boys don't really die they just make rainbows in the sky

(Adored only son of my friends Maureen and Brian)

HEAVEN

Streets are pure gold
In Heaven we are told
Never a tear, no need to fear
The fight has been won
Christ overcome
The city's four square
Loved one's are there
Jesus will say
"Come to me, you are free"
We will hunger no more
Nor thirsty we'll be
The sick, they are healed
The blind they can see!
Heaven is bright there is no night
Light, life and love there
Music and song
The rainbow encircles the throne
We'll be HOME

Tommy

There are many different mental and emotional conditions which include dyspraxia, anorexia, alcoholism, bulimia, obsessive compulsive disorder and depression. Howard Hughes the famous actor himself suffered with o.c.d.

Is there an answer to all the questions we ask? Is there hope? The answer is YES! Progress is being made and more understanding is now available concerning emotional disorder. There is a light at the end of the tunnel. When we are born into this world it is from the darkness of the womb and often there is pain and struggle but it ends with LIFE and light

In Christ we always have hope. He is Alpha and Omega, the beginning and the end.

Genesis, the first book in scripture starts with heaven, light, life, liberty and the RAINBOW. At the cross the price has been paid in blood for our salvation and in Christ we are free.

When we come to the last book of scripture, Revelation we find heaven, life, light, liberty and a rainbow around the throne of the RISEN Christ. He says "I WILL MAKE ALL THINGS NEW".

In Winter-time the field of hope looks desolate but in the Spring-time there is life anew and what we thought was dead is alive.

Edwards Brothers Malloy
Thorofare, NJ USA
July 10, 2015